THEY DIED TOO YOUNG

GLENN MILLER

BY
James Brown

∥∥∥ •PARRAGON• ∥∥∥

This edition first published by Parragon Books Ltd in 1995

Produced by
Magpie Books Ltd, London

Copyright © Parragon Book Service Ltd 1995
Unit 13–17, Avonbridge Trading Estate, Atlantic Road
Avonmouth, Bristol, BS11 9QD

Illustrations courtesy of: Associated Press: Rex Features:
Mary Evans Picture Library: Aquarius Picture Library.

ISBN 0 75250 826 1

A copy of the British Library Cataloguing in Publication
Data is available from the British Library.

Typeset by Hewer Text Composition Services, Edinbur
Printed in Singapore by Printlink International Co.

THEY DIED TOO YOUNG
Glenn Miller

Childhood

The Millers were poor – dirt poor. And at times in the childhood of Alton Glenn Miller the dirt was all too real, as when the family fetched up in the Nebraska Dust Bowl. Those who cavilled in later years at Miller's canny stinginess should have tried living poor in the richest country in the world. It's a tough and toughening way to be raised.

He was born on the first day of March, 1904, in Clarinda, Iowa. His father, Lewis

Elmer Miller, seems to have been an amiable man. He was a carpenter when he could get the work. He was anything else that was going when he couldn't. He had to struggle to put food in his family's mouths. They had to make sacrifices too. For one thing, they had to trail around the vastness of the Midwest as Lewis Miller sought the means to earn a pittance. So in 1909 they moved to Nebraska, into the Dust Bowl, an environmental disaster caused by over-cultivation of the land, too little rain, and too much wind. As the goodness of the land was exhausted, it turned hostile, as the winds lashed the topsoil up into the faces of the swarms of hopeful humanity who looked to it for a living. The Millers were reduced to living in a sod-hut, while Lewis Miller toiled in a town forty miles away.

Young Glenn (he always hated the 'Alton') was soon pressed into service to eke out the family fortunes. He later recalled, 'My first job was milking a cow for two dollars a week.' Other such menial work would fill up the odd hours of his childhood.

The family kept moving about. They lived for a time in Grant City, Missouri. The young Glenn, as ever, tried to help with the family's finances. At one point he worked as a butcher's delivery-boy. One day, downstairs in the butcher's cellar, he happened to notice an oddly shaped, twisted pipe propping up a cupboard. He was intrigued. The kindly butcher explained that it was a trombone, extricated it from his ramshackle cellar, and presented to the young boy.

He also gave the future bandleader a few lessons – though, considering the use to which he'd put the instrument, one cannot help wondering whether they were much use.

There's a kind of rags-to-riches story (one might call it the Cinderella type) in which a poor, undereducated genius suddenly reveals inborn talent of such power that all obstacles melt before it. It would be pleasant to record that Miller's talent was of this type – his temperament might have been the sweeter if it had been. But for him it would be a hard slog. If hard work had been enough to make a trombonist of genius, he'd have been unsurpassed. But the truth is he became no more than a competent player, still plagued by such doubts about is own ability when he became a bandleader that he didn't play at first. Perspiration was always going to carry him further than inspiration.

His was an upbringing to make or break you. You could either absorb the hopeless conviction that whatever you did you wouldn't amount to much; or you could develop an iron determination to put as much distance and cash as possible between yourself and your origins. Miller chose the latter course. Some have argued that his brother Herb went the other way. At any rate, in later years, when Glenn was the most famous bandleader of his day, his brother tried lamely to follow his lead. But, for all Glenn's help, he never made it.

Besides the butcher, Miller's mother also took a hand in his musical education. Mattie Lou Miller was one of those quietly determined women who hold families together in troubled times almost by force of will alone. She drilled young Glenn with the help of a hymnal. That God-fearing sound may not have been much in evidence in the 'Glenn Miller Sound' of later years, but the habits of relentless discipline formed at his mother's knee certainly were.

As soon as he was well able, young Alton Glenn Miller started playing in local concerts. When the family moved again, this time to Fort Morgan, Colorado, he went to high school, somehow finding the time to play the trombone, and make a few dollars doing odd jobs and working part-time in a sugar beet factory. He also indulged a passion for football, into which he threw himself with self-sacrificing gusto. In one match, he played with such unstinting energy that, after the final whistle, it was all he could do to stagger home before crashing out for an hour on the floor.

He even managed to get through his school work – though perhaps only with extra infusions of maternal will-power. He was awarded his diploma, but, since he was unable to collect it in person, his mother received it instead. His headmaster laconically reflected that the award had probably gone to the person who most deserved it.

Marriage

Mattie Lou Miller's encouragement did not suffice to see her son through university. Perhaps her expertise did not extend to the higher curriculum.

At any event, Glenn went up to the University of Colorado. Here he continued to play football. Always intensely competitive, Miller won a place in the all-State team. Later on, in a manner reminiscent of Sir Frank Benson, the actor-manager and ardent amateur sportsman, one recommendation for a job in Miller's outfit was a willingness to play golf with the boss at all hours and in all weathers. However, Miller had none of Benson's genial amateurishness. He personally made time for golf by getting up early: his band as a whole wouldn't have time to play the other bands in their unofficial musicians' league.

Miller was also playing in bands, taking his trombone along to the miscellany of one-night stands, and playing for a while with Boyd Senter at the Albany Hotel, Colorado.

However, ironically (or, perhaps, revealingly), his lacklustre academic record

shows that, while the budding bandleader passed algebra, he failed music. Cal-
culation and precision would characterize
Miller both on the bandstand and off it.

He quit Colorado without taking a
degree, and in November 1925 joined
Ben Pollack's orchestra out on the West
Coast. In a role that would come to be
typical of him, besides playing the horn,
he also made some arrangements. Here
he also ran into a very young Benny
Goodman. Goodman went on to become a bandleader and probably the
most famous clarinettist of the Swing
era — a player of staggering virtuosity,
though also possessed of a personality
which, to put it diplomatically, attracted
mixed comment. When Miller first met
him, Goodman was so young that he

would show up at the venue still wearing his shorts, and would have to go to the locker-room to change into long trousers for the show.

For all his coolly unemotional manner, Miller was in some ways a man of intense and even ungovernable feelings. It would later be a feature of his relations with the guys in his band that they were governed by his initial gut reaction to them. Once Miller had decided he didn't like a man, that was it. He might be rationally disciplined enough to go on employing him if he thought him a good enough musician, but not rationally self-critical enough to question his feelings. Miller dealt in clear-cut verdicts, one way or the other, but without much room for uncertainty in between. He appears to have

Glenn Miller

Glenn Miller with Ray Eberley

had scant ability to live with doubts, which possibly contributed to the calculating side of his nature, which is otherwise difficult to relate to the powerful emotions that would occasionally manifest themselves on the surface. Thus Miller's personality was made up of parts which didn't sit with each other particularly easily. He would guard his inner self with buttoned-down reserve and occasionally with aggression.

How do you get close to such a man?

The one person who unquestionably did was Helen Dorothy Burger. They met while they were both students at university. It would be pleasant to be able to record that it was love at first sight, followed by a whirlwind romance.

Eventually Miller was to become absolutely devoted to her in his uncompromising way, but his powerful feelings were slow to express themselves. Though they met at university, they did not marry until 6 October 1928 – several years later. The gap baffled the future Mrs Miller as much as anyone. In the end it was she who took the initiative, bringing things to a head by raising the possibility of her marrying someone else. That was enough to bring the competitive Miller to the point of proposing – or at least of making it clear that she was *his*, and that he would tolerate no dispute about it. Once the die had been cast, that was it. Given the way Miller's steel-trap mind worked, and arguably reflecting his craving for security, the relationship was irrevocably fixed.

His marriage may have met his need for emotional security. But, although his upbringing in a poor family had left him with a strong need for financial security, the business in which he worked would deny it him for most of his career.

From Pollack's outfit Miller went to join Paul Ash's Paramount Theater Orchestra, and also developed the other side of his career as an arranger.

It was a strange world Miller had moved into. It could be glamorous, but it could also be plain seedy. It could also be dangerous. These were the days of high-profile criminal gangs, some of the most powerful of which would be the ultimate employers of some bands, through their multifarious leisure interests. For example, the drummer Ray McKinley was actually shot by one lot of gangsters – and then the mobsters he worked for picked up his medical expenses. It was while he was recuperating that he went along to hear Pollack's band, and heard his future boss playing trombone for the first time.

Miller cut an odd figure in this milieu. He was described by his lawyer as looking more like a schoolteacher or a clergyman than a musician. And so he did – earnest face, large head, square-cut jaw, athletic, reserved. The work-ethic may not have loomed large on the music scene, but it dominated Miller. Among colleagues for whom recklessness and occasional brilliance were the norm,

Miller was assiduous at practising the trombone. Even so, the verdict of his early colleague, Jimmy McPartland, that he was 'not much of a trombone-player' was a common one, albeit offset by plenty of well-qualified judges who reckon him a fine musician. There was not much spontaneity in Miller's character, and not much in his music either. Individual brilliance would never count for as much in his band as it did in others. Where a different kind of musician would achieve his effect by managing to sound as if he'd just made the whole thing up on the spur of the moment (sometimes, of course, because he really had), the impact of Miller's band was more that of the irresistible and inevitable progress of a well-drilled army on the move – which makes it apt that his last band was part of the military, under the command of Major Miller.

His limitations as player grated with him. In later years, when he had his own outfit, he avoided playing for a time. According to one story, the reason he left Pollack's was all to do with his sensitivity on this point. Apparently Pollack had heard Jack Teagarden playing – and liked what he heard. Teagarden was an extraordinary player who developed techniques by which he coaxed sounds from the horn that few others could manage. Pollack came back full of this. Miller, so the story goes, found an excuse to resign from the band soon afterwards, so making way for Teagarden – though, according to some tellings of the tale, he stayed on for a while as arranger.

There's a story that's sometimes told about Miller which dates from these years, which claims to show that he wasn't the dourly unemotional man he's sometimes been made out to be. The trumpeter, Earl Baker, was getting married. Miller, in the unusual role of practical joker, rearranged the slats of the bed in the Bakers' room so that on their first night of wedded bliss the whole thing collapsed. Some joke. A couple of things might be worth noting about this. For all its slapstick fun, there's a streak of *schadenfreude* in this kind of gag, which leaves the prankster very much in control. And when Miller himself was about to get married, he kept very buttoned up about it. No one was about to play the same trick on him.

Freelancing

The Millers moved to New York. Miller spent some time playing in Paul Ash's Paramount Theater Orchestra. But it was a huge outfit, and not really suited to his taste. Mostly he made his living in the early years of his marriage as a freelance musician and arranger. He also made some recordings, appearing on disc with, among others, the Dorsey Brothers and Bing Crosby.

Miller's success took him and his wife to
New York

Miller made several recordings with
Benny Goodman

Miller may have had his doubts about his abilities as a player, but he soon proved a very useful person to have around. For some five years he put in appearances in the studio by day and in the pit-bands by night. He recorded with Red Nichols and the Five Pennies – Miller later revealed that it was more like the Ten Pennies, because to fill out the sound Nichols would sometimes double up each player with another hidden behind a curtain. Nichols found him 'a very thoughty [*sic*] guy'. Goodman, with whom he also recorded, praised him for being 'a dedicated musican and always so thorough'.

However laudable, this may sound a little soulless. But, as drummer Gene Krupa discovered, there was another side to him. They were both playing in the pit for a show called *Girl Crazy*. Krupa was a fine musician, but at that time he couldn't read music to save his life. This didn't matter when you were playing in a dance band, but for a stage show you played from the score. Miller had naturally mastered reading musical scores along with every other technical aspect of the job. Every night he'd keep his eye on the percussion part as well as his own, and would cue Krupa in. Krupa was eternally grateful to him.

Miller's technical prowess went beyond just reading scores, and increasingly included making them up as an arranger. Here, as elsewhere, he applied himself doggedly to the task. He also leaned on the training he had got from Dr Joseph

Schillinger, who had devised a mathematical approach to harmony. Music does lend itself to this, but it also leaves plenty of room for instinct and artistic impulse and gut feeling. But Miller always liked to go by the numbers. Later he would amuse, or sometimes infuriate, his own arrangers by putting their scores through the mathematical mill before going into rehearsal with them. Not for nothing was this the man who passed algebra at university, but flunked music.

Music wasn't the only area of his life where Miller was into numbers. The numbers game loomed large when it came to money, too – in particular, when it came to being taxed. When his friend, the music journalist George Simon, discussed with Miller the possibility of writing a biography of him he was dismayed to find that Miller seemed to reckon his achievements mostly in terms of dollars. Anyone who sought to take them off him was the enemy. So, for example, in the tax year 1930 Miller earned the handsome sum of $6,239.50 for playing and for making some fifty-one arrangements. By the time he'd made deductions for every last thing he could think of, down to having his suits pressed and buying his buttonholes, his total tax bill came in at just $17.38.

In many ways, Miller's success was as much a matter of business sense as of music. He was somewhat unusual in his world in possessing that kind of acumen. It made him valuable to the likes of Smith Ballew. Ballew was a dashingly good-looking man who fronted his own band largely on the strength of appearance and personality. But he was pretty short in the back-room skills of the job. As Ray McKinley observed, Ballew was too easygoing to be a good bandleader. He later had some success in Hollywood, where looks and personality go somewhat further. However, Ballew was no fool. When he got a deal to play the prestigious Palais Royale, Long Island, he realized that if the date was to do him long-term good, he'd have to get his band into shape, and he knew just the man to do it. Miller was to have $250 a week and a share in the profits for playing, rehearsing and arranging.

This was fine up to a point. But, as Ballew said of Miller: 'He had no social amenities and he preferred to remain in the background. He was definitely an introvert. He was hard to know. He never bared his soul to anyone that I know of.' As the band toured the country, they were often working under some stress. This was in the early thirties, when the after-effects of the Wall Street Crash were still being felt. People didn't have as much spare cash to lavish on music as they might have liked, so there could be long lay-offs between engagements. Some players were mutually supportive. But not Miller. By the end of his time with Ballew, he wasn't even playing with them any more: he just ran the rehearsals and took care of the business.

It was difficult enough to be this remote with a bunch of guys for whom the

The Glenn Miller Band

Performing with the singer Marion Hutton

camaraderie of the road meant a good deal, and for whom being in harmony with each other (and not just in the literal sense) was important. But Miller, with a few drinks inside him, could become just plain mean. Matters came to a head one New Year's Eve in the Muehlbach Hotel in Kansas City, when he got into a regular punch-up with the trumpeter J. D. Wade.

Given that alcohol could have this unpleasant effect on him, it was just as well that, for most of the time, he had enough self-knowledge and self-discipline to lay off the stuff – though not without the help of a lesson from his wife. One time he set off on a massive two-day drunk, in the course of which he drew money from their joint account. When Mrs Miller found out about it, she hit her husband where it hurt: in the wallet. She went on a binge of her own – a clothes-buying binge. Neither of the Millers were people you'd want to get the wrong side of.

After leaving Smith Ballew, Miller got a couple of jobs where his back-room skills were again invaluable. He helped the Dorsey Brothers to assemble a band in 1934, but then got caught in the middle of a huge row between the brothers, as a result of which all three of them – the two Dorseys and Miller – went their separate ways. Then he had a similar task to perform for Ray Noble. Noble had made a name for himself in the States with some recordings he'd made over in England, and he was trying to assemble an American band that would live up to his reputation.

This was all valuable experience for Glenn Miller. Noble, in particular, with his preference for a lyrical, ballad style, made an interesting counterweight to Glenn Miller's jazz-influenced tastes. Even so, Miller was frustrated. Matters came to a head when money was tight and Noble asked the band to take a pay cut. Though Miller could be generous on occasion, bailing out promoters who'd stood by him, and giving bonuses to his crew, he could never tolerate people welching on deals, and he led a walk-out. But, looking back, he later offered a more long-standing motive for quitting: 'I was tired of arguing about arrangements, of having things come out differently from the way I wrote them. I wanted to hear my own ideas and the only way was to have my own crew.'

Band One

Miller had in-depth knowledge of the business and he had some business sense, but, even so, putting together a successful band was a tall order. Miller's first attempt was to fail. Unlike the way today's rock bands often operate, on a profit-share basis, Miller's kind of band typically consisted of a leader who then hired all the players. The overheads of such an operation could break you.

If success had simply been a matter of sheer hard work, then there was no question but Miller was heading for the top. But in show business you've got to be lucky too, no matter how good or industrious you are. Before the good times started to roll, Miller was to stare the possibility of financial ruin in the face. For a man who'd been brought up poor and craved security, it was an alarming prospect. Typically, he faced it down.

The problems that defeated the first venture into band-leading were threefold: the savings-gobbling cost of it, problems over getting bookings, and dissension within the ranks.

Miller had done the obvious thing, and tried to get the best players he could find.

But the most inspired musicians were seldom the most stable characters. The worst of them were chronic boozers. Miller himself forswore the demon drink for most of the time, the better to lead the band. Given his love of discipline, he must often have wished that certain of his players were on the wagon as well – even before the serious soaks on his team managed to write off two cars and a truck.

Some of the guys Miller was trying to keep in line were larger-than-life characters. Irving 'Fazola' Prestopnik, for example. The man had a huge talent for the clarinet, and he also had a huge girth and a huge Falstaffian appetite for liquor to match. Such men play fast and loose with their talent and their health –

and they're also the types to drive managers to nervous collapse.

Miller assigned Jerry Jerome, one of the younger and supposedly more responsible members of the band, to room with Fazola and Bob Price, who was the lead trumpeter and another epic imbiber. Maybe Miller trusted Jerome because he'd been to medical school before taking up music as a career. But the kind of drugs Fazola was into were not primarily for the sake of his health. Deciding one evening to try marijuana instead of booze for a change, Fazola enlisted Jerome's support in the effort to get high. The problem was that Fazola, among his various vices, had never learned to smoke, so inhaling the weed was tricky for him. But Fazola was determined.

Jerome claims he ended up having to put a waste-paper basket over the dissolute clarinette's head, sticking a lit joint inside, and then sealing it in by wrapping wet towels round his neck. Fazola got high – he damn near died, but he got high.

Sometimes even the drunks in the other bands could give Miller's fortunes a knock. One of the great problems Miller had, given his rock-solid, mathematical sense of rhythm, was getting his bands to really swing. That depends on subtle irregularities in the beat, best felt by intuition, and by a bunch of musicians who are feeling laid-back. It wasn't that his tempi were slow – if anything, he was inclined to drive through numbers like an express train. But it don't mean a thing if

it ain't got that swing – and Miller was
too sharp not to know it. He thought
maybe a new drummer would help.
Good luck struck when Tommy Dorsey
lent Glenn his drummer, Maurice Purtill.
It was an improvement; Purtill had flair.
But then Dorsey's other drummer went
on a huge alcoholic bender, so Purtill had
to be returned to sender (though he
subsequently signed up for a later Glenn
Miller Band). After a brief burst of
percussive prowess, it was back to the
old ways for the Miller Band.

On one occasion, Miller went for an
effect that required total coordination –
the kind of thing that would later lend
such showmanship to his work. He
devised an arrangement of 'Danny
Boy', which brought in the band section

Playing for a dance in the film *Orchestra Wives*

The successful band leader

by section, brass first. He thought it would be a stylish move to start in darkness and then have each section picked out by a spotlight as it came in. Nice idea. Except that when it came to show-time, the spot hit the reeds first, who sat there looking non-plussed, while the horns blared away in the darkness.

Other of his ploys made fine sense in commercial terms, if not in musical ones. For example, at one session the band found themselves backing a singer whose sense of pitch was less than perfect. But Miller the businessman knew what he was about: she was the daughter of an NBC executive, and Miller was angling for air time. Then again, in New Orleans the band found themselves playing a new, but somewhat pedestrian, piece in each evening's set. Once more, dollar-wise (and dollar-anxious) Miller had his reasons: the song was by a local entrepreneur who owned a string of bars. There he was every night, bringing yet another group of his friends and relations to admire his handiwork.

Miller was losing money hand-over-fist. As if professional misfortunes were not enough, his private life was marred by misfortune too. Helen Miller suffered an illness which caused her to be rushed to hospital. Agonizingly for them, the upshot was that they would never be able to have children of their own. One might suppose that, for so notoriously unemotional a man, this would not be as great a loss as it would be for most folk. But that's to confuse a man's not showing his feelings with his not having them. Miller had them all right – he had them bottled up, corked and sealed. For some years the Millers diverted their parental care in the direction of 'Pops', a Boston bull-terrier. When the dog died Miller cracked up, completely grief-stricken. later on, Maurice Purtill rejoined Miller's band in its second incarnation. At a hotel one day, Purtill left his five-year-old son by the hotel pool in the care of a friend. He was alarmed, then, to see his friend wander into the bar. He ran to the pool, half-expecting to see his little boy floating face-downwards. But no – he was playing happily with Glenn Miller. In fact, they were both playing happily with each other, even though Purtill junior was impertinetly advising

Miller to play more like Tommy Dorsey.

There were some useful by-products of the first band – principally, perhaps, the discovery of one of the keys to the Miller sound. Fazola was a genius on the clarinet, but no great shakes on the sax. So, partly just to keep the big guy's mind on the job, Miller scored the sax parts with Fazola doubling them on the clarinet. Even after Fazola had gone on to induce chronic anxiety in other managements, Miller kept the sound.

Even so, the first venture into management had been miserable, and financially disastrous. On New Year's Eve 1937, Miller gave the band their notice.

With his wife Helen and their son

Major Glenn Miller

The Glenn Miller Band

At this low point, Glenn Miller seems to have contemplated abandoning his dream of leading a band entirely. Yet his feelings were mixed. After the band broke up, and before Miller had even admitted to himself that he was going to start another, George Simon helped Jerry Jerome land himself another job. He was taken aback when a touchy Miller interpreted this as a personal betrayal, a misconception from which he was only weaned by degrees.

Hal MacIntyre witnessed Miller's change of heart. MacIntrye had been in the first band. Some time after it had folded, Miller and himself met for a chat and a coffee in a diner. At the start of their conversation, Miller was adamant: he was out of the band-leading, wallet-emptying business. By the end of it, he had scheduled the first rehearsal for the new band in the Haven Studio the following week.

Miller had learned a lesson from the first band: 'One thing I definitely won't have this time is some of those prima donnas.' Teamwork was a trump individual flair every time in the new outfit. He kept a few players from the first band, mostly the younger ones. Willie Schwartz, for example, was a fine reedsman, who looked up to Miller as a father-figure. Miller ran

the new crew almost like scout camp.
Hair was to be regulation length, shoes
were to shine, uniforms were to be
pressed, and exactly the same quantity
of white handkerchief was to peek from
each man's top pocket. As Miller explained, 'Anybody gets out of line, and
out he goes.'

In spite of this austere regime, Miller
elicited not just respect but love from
some of his players. Tex Beneke, a young
saxophonist whom Miller brought to the
fore as a singer partly on account of his
winning personality, was one such. A
later addition to the line-up, the bassist
Trigger Alpert, also got on well with
Miller, who perhaps regarded him as
something of a surrogate son. The
band's main *chanteuse*, Marion (sister of

Betty) Hutton, was just a teenager when she joined, so she naturally looked up to Miller, who, because she was a minor, became her legal guardian.

Even to the favoured, Miller could be unforthcoming. Hutton's looks and personality made her a huge draw, but she was no great singer, and smart enough to know it. She desperately wanted to please Miller, so, in advance of one recording date, she secretely took lessons from Mimi Spier. With nervous anticipation, she looked forward to surprising Miller. He was surprised all right, but once he'd got over it his only comment was 'knock off the goddamn lessons. I want you to sing like Marion Hutton'. Understandably she felt crushed.

Miller was sometimes readier to show his feelings by actions rather than words. For his favourite, Tex Beneke, no trouble was too much, even if it meant bending his own rules – provided, of course, that Miller could contrive it so he didn't look like he was bending them. When the band was a huge hit, Beneke was voted one of the top players in the country, and was invited, along with the other poll-toppers, to play a date as an All-Star Band. The problem was that it clashed with a booking of the Glenn Miller Band at the Café Rouge. As a matter of principle Miller couldn't just let Tex off for the evening, so he privately told Beneke to show up at the Café Rouge, and then make a big enough show of bellyaching about something to give him an excuse to send him off the stand in time for the All-

Star session. So Beneke started grousing,
and Miller, with a convincing show of
annoyance, told him to get the hell out of
it. But at this point, Ernie Caceres loyally
leapt to Tex's defence and announced, 'If
he goes, I go too'. With some difficulty,
and doubtless seething inside, Miller
finally managed to get Caceres back in
his seat, and Beneke away for his session.

Other kindnesses were more above-
board. For example, it happened that
Chuck Goldstein, one of the four Mod-
ernaires, who formed part of the band's
singing strength, heard that his father had
had a stroke. He arrived home, but too
late – his father was dead. When he flew
back to rejoin the band in Washington,
Glenn Miller took him out after the show.
'I'll never forget that night,' Goldstein

Miller's band travelled to London on the *Queen Elizabeth*

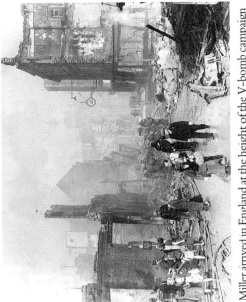

Miller arrived in England at the height of the V-bomb campaign

recalled. 'Nobody could have been kinder or more thoughtful than Glenn was then.'

Even those who didn't get on well with him could find that their boss was a friend of much practical kindness in a crisis. Al Klink was a fine reeds-player, whom Miller had recruited by rousing at four o'clock one morning (Miller was driving back to New York from New England after a show). But, despite Miller's apparent enthusiasm to have Klink in the band, Klink never felt fully accepted: Miller neither praised him, nor drew him out as a player, as was to happen later when he played with Benny Goodman. And yet, when Klink's mother was invovled in a car accident, it was Miller who immediately set about making travel arrangements to speed Klink to his mother's side.

The new band made slow progress. Miller had financed it with a second mortgage on his in-law's house. They got through 1938 with some less than prestigious, and at times downright sleazy, bookings. By the end of the year, Miller was again thinking of throwing in the towel. All the band had brought him at the bank was debts. He'd even had to borrow a couple of thousand dollars from Tommy Dorsey, which later led to a falling out, because Dorsey was under the misapprehension that he'd bought a piece of the band, and carried his pique to the extreme lengths of starting up a whole new band on purpose to mimic Miller's style.

At this low point, the Boston entrepreneur Cy Shribman stepped in to bail Miller out. He took on the band's debts, which probably stood at $10–12,000, and arranged some dates. Shribman cut an unusual figure on the Boston scene. He managed his interests on the hoof, hastening from venue to venue of an evening, disbursing and collecting quantities of cash, which he kept stuffed in his pockets. It looked erratic, but he must have had some special pocket-money system of his own, because, though he never took any notes, his books were always in order.

The band eventually got its big break when it landed a booking at the Glen Island Casino. It was a prestigious place to play. Not only was there a young trendsetting audience in the Casino, but there was an NBC radio link which flashed the hot sounds of fashionable night-life around the networks.

They made their début on 17 May 1939. From the first, they were a sensation. 'It was a phenomenon the way the guy hit,' recalls drummer Moe Purtill. That distinctive reeds sounds with the clarinet over the saxes, the extraordinary energy and precision of the playing, the visual fun of the meticulous choreography with the horns all moving in sync and saxes swinging together – all these hallmarks of their style were essentially Miller's own ideas. The Glenn Miller Band were fine musicians, and they became fine showmen.

For Glen Island they went on a kind of triumphal progress, breaking box office records as they went. The Baltimore Hippodrome had never known crowds like Glenn Miller drew in the first week of September 1939. And they played three weeks at the Paramount Theater in New York with the Ink Spots. Not only that, but Miller managed to land the lucrative and conspicious Chesterfield cigarette radio – commerical spot, which would routinely bring the sounds of the band to the air waves.

At long last, Miller was making money. Going back to dates he'd played before the Glen Island sensation, he found he commanded fees up to ten times what he'd been getting before. And he was much in demand. In fact, he had almost too much to do. There was one two-week period in which, what with the Chesterfield shows (which all went out live), and performances at the Paramount, as well as appearances at the Pennyslvania Hotel, the band gave 140 performances. As Tex Beneke recalled, the horns wouldn't have time to get cold between one show and the next, and scarcely saw the inside of their cases.

The pressure was hard on Miller. He found himself having to try to get out of doing things he felt he ought to be doing, simply because he lacked the time. At one point, he confided to George Simon that he didn't much care for the person he was becoming, but then again, 'Maybe a guy in my position can't be the person he wants to be'. It's possible he

The bomber crew which may have destroyed Miller's plane

Glenn Miller's memorial on Hollywood's Walk of Fame

never really enjoyed his success. Polly
Davis, a close friend of the Millers, who
ran Miller's office for him, said, 'He had
had so many knocks that when the money
finally started coming in, he watched it
very carefully – so carefully in fact, that I
don't think he ever truly enjoyed having
it.' It all took its toll on his health, which
finally landed him in Mount Sanai Hospital suffering from 'flu, sinus infection
and exhaustion. Old friends in the business showed the esteem in which they
held him by standing in for him while the
band continued on its hectic schedule.

Attendance records continued to tumble,
and records of the other sort continued to
sell, as Miller reached the disc-buying
public via RCA Victor. This was the
man who, not many years before, hadn't

been able to land a recording contract. When, at last, a long-running dispute cleared the way for Miller to record 'Chantanooga Choo Choo', it sold, and it sold, and it sold – one million, two hundred thousand times it sold. No recording had ever sold so many copies before. Casting about for a way to honour their star, RCA Victor hit upon the idea of presenting him with a pressing of his money-spinner in gold. So Glenn Miller became the recipient of the first ever gold disc.

Hollywood wanted a piece of the Miller action, too; and so they headed west to make, first of all, *Sun Valley Serenade*, and then, in late spring of 1942, *Orchestra Wives*.

Miller's War

It was on the train on the way back to Chicago after shooting *Orchestra Wives* that rumours started to buzz around the band that their leader was contemplating signing up for an entirely different kind of shooting.

With the outbreak of the Second World War, it became likely that sooner or later the US would be lured into battle. The prospect depressed Miller. Not because he was unpatriotic – quite the reverse. Even before the US entered the conflict, Miller started doing 'Sunset Serenade', a special radio series designed to boost the morale of the services. Each week five army camps would decide on their favourite number. Miller would then play all five on the show, and poll the audience. The camp whose song came out top would receive a radio-phonograph and fifty assorted records. Each show cost Miller about $1,000, because he paid for these gifts out of his own pocket.

The band's success continued to be immense, even though Uncle Sam was starting to claim some of its members for the draft. Miller himself was too old to be called up. But though he had a hugely successful business to run, and

Ray McKinley briefs the Glenn Miller Band

James Stewart and June Allyson in the *Glenn Miller Story*

could fairly be thought to be doing his bit for the country, Miller had no intention of hanging back. As he explained, 'I, like every American, have an obligation to fulfil. That obligation is to lend as much support as I can to winning this war. It is not enough for me to sit back and buy bonds . . . I sincerely feel I owe a debt of gratitude to my country . . .' He registered for the draft on 15 February 1942. Then, that June, he secretly applied to the US Naval Reserve for a commission. No dice: on 1 August, they turned him down.

Finally, via his friend Brigade General Charles D. Young, he managed to persuade the military that his talents could be of immense value in morale-building. He was accepted to train to become Captain A. Glenn Miller.

But before that, he had to say so long to the band. He broke the news to them while they were working on one of the Chesterfield broadcasts. Their final performance was to be at the Central Theater, Passaic, New Jersey, on 29 September 1942. Everyone was emotional – even the stoical Miller. Somehow they made it to their final number. But then Marion Hutton broke down in tears and had to leave the stage. The audience were in no better condition. Overcome by emotion, Miller made the mistake of turning away from the band, only to behold a sea of faces awash with tears: 'I could stand everything, all the heartache of breaking up things that had taken years to build – but I just couldn't face those kids.' He followed Marion Hutton off into the wings.

Though he went in for military precision, Miller and the army didn't get on too well at first. His morale wilted under the standard training, followed by his health, which landed him for a while in Fort Meade Hospital. But he was no quitter, and on 4 December 1942 became a captain.

Though he'd signed up for the army, the air force managed to get hold of him. They filed a routine request for the transfer of Capt. Alton G. Miller, and by the time the army realized that this anonymous-looking character was *the* Glenn Miller it was too late.

Although the branches of the service competed to get hold of him, that didn't mean to say that his superiors necessarily welcomed him when they got him. Miller felt frustrated and blocked by unsympathetic superiors, some of whom resented the presence of this famous, wealthy man. Worse than that, Miller was there expressly to overhaul the army's music, and some old hands hated that. At one point Miller's frustrations overflowed in a letter to Lt. Col. Richard E. Daley: '. . . if we are persistently heckled by various higher authorities for trying to do the job as best we know, my own personal desire would be to forget about the whole thing and to get into some routine military function where this opposition wouldn't be ever-present.'

If Miller was having problems with the military life, the men he was recruiting to his outfit weren't having it much easier. At least Miller was a born disciplinarian, but the musicans he gathered around him were anything but. The pianist Mel Powell tells a story of going out on a parade in which he was assigned to play glockenspiel or some such. He became quite absorbed in this. Order came to turn, and he turned. After a while, he thought, 'What a beautiful diminuendo the guys are doing' only to look up and find that it wasn't that they were playing more and more quietly, but that where he'd turned left, they'd all turned right, and were now several blocks away. Powell ducked into the nearest bar.

Then again, there was another pianist who'd got his kittens with him in the camp. He was so fond of them he couldn't bear to leave them, even when he went out on parade. So if you found yourself marching alongside Pte. Arnold, you'd hear muffled miaows coming from inside his tunic.

These unlikely soldiers, whether the army liked it or not, were doing good work. They played for war-bond drives; from July 1943 they played the 'I Sustain the Wings' radio show, which soon became the most popular show on air, and helped with recruitment; and generally they boosted morale. The soldiers who marched to Miller's beat were marching to music of a type that meant something to *them*, if not to their fathers. A good army may be an obedient one, but no one fights well just because they're told to – the heart's got to be in it. Heart-stirring was the job Miller had set himself.

It was inevitable that he should seek to get into the war zone – for where else was good morale more necessary? Yet there was more than ever to keep him in the States, for he finally had a family: the Millers had managed to adopt a baby boy, whom Miller absolutely adored. But he was clear as to where his duty lay. He pulled strings to get orders to go, and on 18 June 1944 he set off for London. The AAF Band was directed to follow on via 'NY8245', which turned out to be army-speak for the liner *Queen Elizabeth*.

They found a war-scarred London that was having to cope with Hitler's terrifying V-bombs. Briefly billeted at 25

Sloane Court, Miller had them all moved out to work up in Bedford. They grumbled at the time, because they'd hoped to spend their first Sunday looking around the town. When later a V-bomb hit near by, killing twenty-five and demolishing the building, they were glad they'd moved.

In fact, they kept on moving. Miller drove them at a furious pace. They flew all around Britain, playing at airfields and bases everywhere; they played in war-bond drives; they played on the radio every day. Sometimes the huge band divided its forces, to produce a dance band led by Ray McKinley and a seven-piece jazz band led by Mel Powell. And they won a lot of fans. General Dolittle expressed his gratitude to him, saying, 'Captain Miller, next to a letter from home, your band's the greatest boost to morale in the European theater of Operations.' The Commander-in-Chief himself, General Dwight Eisenhower, expressed his gratitude. But it wasn't just Americans a long way from home who relished the Miller Military Sound. The British loved it too. Don Haynes, a friend of Miller's who had worked for him before the war, and was now helping to run the AAF Band, met the Queen (now the Queen Mother), who praised the band's work, and revealed that 'the Princess Elizabeth and Margaret Rose are avid fans of the Glen Miller Band and listen to your nightly broadcasts over the wireless regularly'.

Miller was doing good work – such good work that he was promoted that August. But Major Miller wasn't a happy man. Bill Finegan, who'd been an arranger for his band back in the States, recalls his saying just before he joined up, 'I'm going into this thing, but I don't think I'm coming back'. In Britain this fatalistic mood gained on him. He became homesick as he thought of his wife and son, and the daughter they had also adopted whom he had never seen. He made plans for his life after the war, and had a model built of 'Tuxedo Junction', the house he intended to build on the ranch he'd bought in California. On one occasion, as he indulged his pipedreams in the company of George Voutsas, he suddenly broke off: 'Christ, I don't know why I spend time making plans like this. You know, George, I have an awful feeling you guys are going to go home without me, and I'm going to get mine in some goddamn beat-up old plane.' In November, after uncharacteristically losing to Don Haynes at poker, he returned to the theme: 'Don, I have a strong feeling that I'll never see Helen and Stevie again. I know that sounds odd, but I've had that feeling for some time now. You know the Miller luck has been phenomenal for the last five years, and I don't want to be around when it changes.'

Even so, duty came first. Though he was unhappy and sick with either nerves or some second sight into the future (depending on how you want to look at it), he sought the chance to follow the liberating armies into France. On 15 November he was summoned to Paris, and asked to bring the band to France. In order to go to France, the band had to record their radio programmes in advance, so they could still be heard each day in the ether. So, starting on 25 November and ending on 12 December, they recorded scores and scores of half-hour shows – this in addition to their existing heavy schedule, and to playing the normal nightly radio shows.

Glen Miller's flight was scheduled for 13 December. But the weather was abominable. A fog had descended that was so dense that the London buses had to be guided around the streets by their conductors walking in front of them with a torch. The flight was cancelled. However,

Don Haynes had made the acquaintance of a Colonel Baesell, who was on General Goodrich's staff. Baesell was going to Paris in the General's private plane, so he offered Haynes a lift. Haynes was committed to going over with the rest of the band a few days later, but suggested that perhaps Glenn Miller could take advantage of the Colonel's offer.

Glenn seems, by this time, to have been anxious to be on the move. He seized his chance. Haynes and Miller travelled up from London to Bedford on 14 December to meet the flight, and that evening, they talked into the small hours. The following morning the weather was still vile, but the word was that it might clear that afternoon, so they headed out to the airfield at

Twinwood Farm. The rain curses down; the clouds are low. Flight Lieutenant Morgan is having to fly down from Goodrich's HQ, though in this weather Miller doubts he'll be able to find the field much less get them to France. When he drones overhead and overshoots, these fears seem to be confirmed. But soon they hear him circling back: somehow he's found them.

There are different stories about Miller's last moments on earth. Mel Powell tells a version in which several of the guys in the band, including himself, are on the airfield ready to go with the CO; when Miller hears that the pilot intends to fly low, under the clouds, he decided to lighten the load a little by leaving them behind. It's also said that, as he made to get in, he asked Baesell, 'Where the hell are the parachutes?', only to get the reply, 'What's the matter, Miller? You want to live for ever?'

The C-64 took off into the murky afternoon. Glenn Miller was never seen again.

The band flew over on 18 December. They were disturbed not to be met by their CO, but go on with their job. Ray McKinley recalls that, up to a couple of months afterwards, they still expected Glenn Miller to turn up. Helen Miller spent the rest of her life with a bed made up just in case her husband returned. She was notified on 23 December that he was missing in flight; ironically, it was only five days later that her husband's last message reched her with the delivery of a radio-phonograph which he had planned some time before as a surprise Christmas present.

The band went ahead and followed their leader's plans, playing their first show in liberated France on 21 December, and eventually following the liberating armies into Germany, where they entertained (among others) the Russians. They eventually docked back in New York in August 1945, and gave one final concert in the National Press Club. In the audience were Generals Eisenhower and Arnold, and President Truman. The band's spot was introduced by a moving tribute to their leader from Eddie Cantor. As the curtains swung apart to reveal Glenn

Miller's unit, President Truman led a standing ovation.

The best guess is that Glenn Miller died *en route* to France that filthy December afternoon. It was freezing cold, and, by some oversight, the C-64 carried no de-icing equipment. The inglorious truth may well be that human error killed one of the great stars of the era. It's also been suggested that the plane might have been destroyed in error by a returning bomber squadron which had been unable to find its target, and let loose its payload over the Channel, accidentally killing Miller in the process!

Glenn Miller lives on, of course, in that glorious sound, which epitomizes the whole era. And for the man himself?

Not an easy man to get to know, or an easy man to like. But, overwhelmingly, those who did know him are proud to have done so. That's a fair epitaph for any man.

FURTHER MINI SERIES INCLUDE

THEY DIED TOO YOUNG

Elvis
James Dean
Buddy Holly
Jimi Hendrix
Sid Vicious
Marc Bolan
Ayrton Senna
Marilyn Monroe
Jim Morrison

THEY DIED TOO YOUNG

Malcolm X
Kurt Cobain
River Phoenix
John Lennon
Glenn Miller
Isadora Duncan
Rudolph Valentino
Freddie Mercury
Bob Marley

FURTHER MINI SERIES
INCLUDE

HEROES OF THE WILD WEST

General Custer
Butch Cassidy and the Sundance Kid
Billy the Kid
Annie Oakley
Buffalo Bill
Geronimo
Wyatt Earp
Doc Holliday
Sitting Bull
Jesse James